SO YOU'RE
40!

Mike Haskins & Clive Whichelow

Illustrations by Andy Hammond

summersdale

SO YOU'RE 40!

First published in 2007
Second edition published in 2008
This edition copyright © Mike Haskins and Clive Whichelow, 2013

Illustrations by Andy Hammond

Mike Haskins and Clive Whichelow have asserted their right to be identified as the authors of this work in accordance with sections 77 and 78 of the Copyright, Designs and Patents Act 1988.

Summersdale Publishers Ltd
46 West Street
Chichester
West Sussex
PO19 1RP
UK

www.summersdale.com

Printed and bound in China

ISBN: 978-1-84953-437-6

Substantial discounts on bulk quantities of Summersdale books are available to corporations, professional associations and other organisations. For details contact Nicky Douglas by telephone: +44 (0) 1243 756902, fax: +44 (0) 1243 786300 or email: nicky@summersdale.com.

To.............................

From.........................

INTRODUCTION

So you've made it! You're in your forties! Congratulations!

Finally, you're a proper grown-up. OK, in many parts of the world and at many previous ages in history, 40 would represent your total life expectancy. But don't worry about those doom-mongers who tell you it's all downhill physically and mentally from now on. What the hell do those so-called fully qualified doctors and other medical experts know anyway? And don't worry that deep down inside you know you haven't really matured one iota since you were 15. Life, they say, begins at 40. Obviously that's blatantly untrue. But it is a thing people (often around the age of 40) say to one another.

You've got everything to look forward to, they say. Obviously that's blatantly untrue as well. Realistically speaking you've got about half of everything to look forward to. But seeing as you've reached 40 without anything much ever happening to you, you can now get on with the best half of your life armed with this little book – the ideal primer to what is surely destined to be the greatest decade of your entire life.

THE BASIC MYTHS ABOUT TURNING 40

Maturity has at last made you a fount of knowledge and wisdom – what a pity no one's the least bit interested in listening to you any more

Now you're 40 you have the face you deserve – if so, I'd demand a retrial

DRESS CODE FOR THE OVER 40S – SOME DOS & DON'TS

*Don't try to squeeze
into any trousers you have
owned for more than two
years – not only will you look
ridiculous, there will also
be a significant chance
of asphyxiation*

Don't think anyone wants to see your midriff

*Don't turn to transvestism
at this stage of your life –
it will only emphasise any
problems you already have*

Do learn to laugh at yourself – at least you can beat everyone else to it

TIPS ON HOW TO LOOK YOUNGER THAN YOU ACTUALLY ARE

Avoid the following: all-night parties, drinking, drugs, one-night stands... or basically all the things young people do

Learn to send a text message in less than 20 minutes

Attach a very large bulldog clip to the back of your head to help smooth out all the wrinkles

GIVEAWAYS THAT WILL TELL PEOPLE YOU ARE OVER 40

When someone
asks you to burn a
CD, you reach for
the matches

You complain
about graffiti

*You end text
messages with
'Yours sincerely'*

A GUIDE TO HOW OTHERS WILL NOW PERCEIVE YOU

By old ladies at bus stops: as someone who is not as likely to nick their bag

By children:
as a source of
pocket money

By older people: as someone who now agrees with their more extreme opinions

THE MAIN EVENTS IN YOUR LIFE YOU WILL NOW LOOK FORWARD TO

Going to see your favourite band who have come back on a reunion tour

No longer having to stay in fashion

And best of all – only ten years now till you can book a Saga holiday!

THE MAIN
EVENTS IN YOUR
LIFE THAT ARE
LESS EASY TO
LOOK FORWARD
TO

Going to see your favourite band who have come back on a reunion tour and realising you didn't actually like them that much at the time

The first time clothes from your youth come back into fashion

The first time your children announce they've been studying something that happened in your lifetime in the history lesson at school

CONVERSING WITH YOUNG PEOPLE (PART 1)

*What you say and
what they hear*

'So, what sort of music
do you like?' =
'I desperately need to find
out what's cool because I'm
completely out of touch with
what's going on'

'OK, kids. Who wants a game of football?' =
'Let me show off in front of you and your friends for ten minutes before I keel over and lie on the ground gasping for breath'

NOW
YOU'RE 40 THE
FOLLOWING WILL
BE YOUR NATURAL
ENEMIES

Anyone in a bigger car than yours

Gravity

Your waistband

Next door's cat

A LIST OF CONTROVERSIAL OPINIONS YOU WILL NOW BE EXPECTED TO HOLD

'Anyone caught wearing a baseball cap while at the wheel of a car should be stripped of their licence'

'The police should be entitled to use tasers on anyone who swears in a public place'

CONVERSING WITH YOUNG PEOPLE (PART 2)

*What they say and
what you hear*

**'Mummy/Daddy! Will
you have a game on the
computer with me?' =
'Mummy/Daddy! Can
I thrash you on the
computer?'**

'Mummy/Daddy! Where do babies come from?' = 'Mummy/Daddy! I'd like to watch you squirm with embarrassment for the next ten minutes'

'Trick or treat' =
'Give me some sweets or
me and Dracula here'll
mug you'

THINGS YOU CAN NOW GET AWAY WITH THAT YOU COULDN'T PREVIOUSLY

Talking to an 18-year-old without them thinking you're trying to chat them up

Pulling the bin out to the front of your house while only dressed in your pyjamas

THINGS YOU SHOULD HAVE ACHIEVED BY NOW

*Being able to say
'Uranus' without giggling
and making a puerile joke*

Wearing sunglasses only when it's sunny

The ability to have a good time regardless of how miserable the rest of your family are looking during a day out

THINGS
THAT YOU WILL
TAKE A SUDDEN
INTEREST IN

*The fact that the BBC
also has Radios 2,
3 and 4*

Adverts containing the words 'younger', 'rejuvenate' and 'free'

The best route by road from your house to anywhere else in the country

Your cholesterol level

THINGS YOU'LL FEEL SMUG ABOUT

*Still having
20/20 vision*

The amount you recycle compared to the amount next door have sticking out of the top of their wheelie bin

Making it through the night without having to get up and go to the toilet

BEING 40 IS...

… being too old for nightclubs but too young for nightcaps

... *being too old to be hip and too young for a hip replacement*

... being too old to be looked after by your parents and too young to be looked after by your kids – you're on your own, mate!

THINGS YOU SHOULD NOT HAVE IN YOUR HOME

*Love letters from
all your exes*

Your own superhero outfit (no – not even a crotchless one)

YOUR NEW
OUTLOOK
ON LIFE

Your idea of a busy weekend is doing the shopping and washing the car

Your idea of life in the fast lane is queuing at the 'Five items or fewer' checkout in the supermarket

THINGS YOU WON'T BE DOING ON HOLIDAY ANY MORE

*Being drunk
in charge of a
windsurf board*

*Wearing a swimsuit
only slightly larger
than an elastic band*

REASONS TO BE CHEERFUL

*You're no longer
defined by what
trainers you wear*

Despite the extraordinary amount of environmental damage wreaked on it, planet Earth will probably just about see you out now

You're now old
enough to have a
toy boy/girl

You're mature at last – and if anyone disagrees you'll give them a Chinese burn

If you're interested in finding out more about our books, find us on Facebook at Summersdale Publishers and follow us on Twitter at @Summersdale.

www.summersdale.com